Especially for my late Grandad Jerry Pinkney.
Even though you're not here to see this book, I know you're proud of me.
Light, love, and elevation to your spirit.

Educators and librarians, for a variety of teaching tools, visit us at RHTeachersLibrarians.com • *Library of Congress Cataloging-in-Publication Data*
Name: Pinkney Barlow, Charnelle, author, illustrator. Title: Little Rosetta and the talking guitar : the musical story of Sister Rosetta Tharpe, the woman who invented rock and roll / written and illustrated by Charnelle Pinkney Barlow. • Description: New York : Doubleday Books for Young Readers, 2023. | Audience: Ages 4–7 | Summary: "A picture book biography of pioneering guitarist Sister Rosetta Tharpe" —Provided by publisher.
Identifiers: LCCN 2022013367 (print) | LCCN 2022013368 (ebook) | ISBN 978-0-593-57106-4 (hardcover) | ISBN 978-0-593-57107-1 (library binding) | ISBN 978-0-593-57108-8 (ebook) • Subjects: LCSH: Tharpe, Rosetta, 1915–1973—Juvenile literature. | Guitarists—United States—Biography—Juvenile literature. | Gospel musicians—United States—Biography—Juvenile literature. | Blues musicians—United States—Biography—Juvenile literature. | LCGFT: Picture books. • Classification: LCC ML3930.T425 P55 2023 (print) | LCC ML3930.T425 (ebook) | DDC 787.87166092 [B]—dc23/eng/20220321
MANUFACTURED IN CHINA • 10 9 8 7 6 5 4 3 2 1 • First Edition • Random House Children's Books supports the First Amendment and celebrates the right to read.

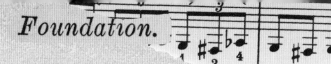

Little Rosetta
AND THE TALKING GUITAR

The Musical Story of Sister Rosetta Tharpe,
the Woman Who Invented Rock and Roll

Written and illustrated by
Charnelle Pinkney Barlow

Doubleday Books for Young Readers

Little Rosetta loved music.
She loved listening to Momma
strum proudly on her mandolin.

zum, zumm, zumm

The notes held her.

A warm hug on Sunday morning.

Every week, the people of Cotton Plant, Arkansas,

joined together to sing and shout.

"Music is the heart of our story," Momma boasted.

Boom, clash, plunk

The pulse of the drums and the tap of the keys

moved Little Rosetta.

Clappin' and twirlin', dancin' and singin'.

"This little light of miiine . . . ," Rosetta belted

to the beat.

One day, Momma surprised her with a special gift.

"Now you can make your very own story," she said.

Little Rosetta placed the guitar on her lap,

drew her hand back, and . . .

Ga-lupp, plink, puh-latz

Notes tumbled out, puzzle pieces waiting to be put together.

"Momma, this guitar is broken," she stated in a huff.

"It looks mighty fine to me. Let's try again, one string at a time."

Guh-lug, thummmm, ker-plunk

Notes wobbled through the air as Little Rosetta carefully plucked each string.

With a satisfied grin, she began practicing, eager to create a story to share at the church anniversary.

Little Rosetta took her guitar everywhere she went, copying the sounds she heard around her neighborhood.

The steady **whirrrrr** of Mrs. Lee's sewing machine.

The sharp **clank** of pots and pans at Mr. Hay's restaurant.

The smooth **rummmmm** of
Miss Waverly's vacuum.

Day after day, Little Rosetta practiced.

Zim, zonk, ver-ummm

She strummed and picked

and plucked some more

until her fingers were as

red as ripe raspberries.

"You're going to wear your fingers
to the bone," warned Momma.

Night after night, soulful rhythms danced through
Little Rosetta's head.

She drifted off to the steady sway of the chords,
with dreams of music flowing from her fingers.
Heavy and sweet like blackberry syrup.

"Tomorrow's another day," Momma whispered
as she kissed Little Rosetta good night.

Fall blew into winter, and winter melted into spring.

Slowly the wobbly notes started to sound like music.

Deeee, duhh, deeeeeeee

The vibrations hummed through her body like bees through a garden.

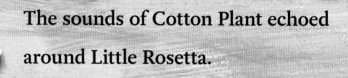

The sounds of Cotton Plant echoed around Little Rosetta.

The low **gruumm** of a train rolling along the tracks.

The sharp **squeeeak** of wagon wheels.

The **buzz** of a crowded market.

She plucked string after string, excited to match the town's song.

Rosetta's upbeat melodies
found folks near and far.

Myles quit his fussin',
Daisy snapped her fingers,
Mrs. Conners hummed a little tune,
and Mr. Thompson couldn't help but tap his toes.

Little Rosetta's confidence grew as her fingers gained speed.

Her fingers hopped around like corn in a kettle.

Wrapping and rolling, billowing and falling,

the music carried her.

Deeeee, dah, dummmmm

Thumm, thummm, POP!

She played until a string snapped, and even that didn't stop her.

Snip, zipppp, zinggggg

"Good as new," said Pastor Murray

(mender of souls and mender of guitars), and off Rosetta went.

"Soundin' good!"
shouted James.

"That's some fast finger pickin',"
snapped Miss Mable.

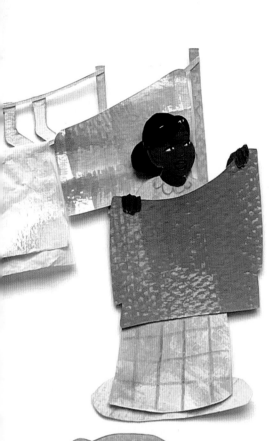

"Gettin' better by the day, I see!"
exclaimed Mr. Walker.

Spring blossomed into summer, and it was time for the church anniversary.

Listening to the adults sing and play, Little Rosetta knew it was her turn to shine.

All eyes were on her.

As she looked out at the hopeful churchgoers,
her calm courage turned to jumpy jellybeans.
She glanced at Momma.

Taking a deep breath,
Little Rosetta picked up her guitar,
drew her hand back, and . . .

Brrummmmmmmmm, dumm, dummm

A joyful noise rose through the air.

"That's my baby." Momma Bell smiled quietly,

strumming a supporting melody on her mandolin.

Little Rosetta wove her music with the sounds around her.

Deeee, dah, duh, dum

Zumm, zummm, thummmm

The notes poured over the crowd like summer rain washing the dust off a new day.

As she got older, time put many miles between Little Rosetta
and Cotton Plant, Arkansas.

She traveled the world, but the music of a small country church
went right along with her.

She wove it into the sounds she found in nightclubs
and created a new form of music.

She came to be known as Sister Rosetta Tharpe: the Godmother of Rock and Roll.

No man alive could make a guitar talk like Sister Rosetta.

The mellow **wooWWW, wahh, wahhh** told of her struggles,

and the bright **zingggg, zang, zing** sang of her triumphs.

For over fifty years, Sister Rosetta played until no more sound could be squeezed from her strings.

Her guitar spoke of the wisdom passed down through generations. The joy and trials of those who came before her.

Music held the story of her people.

And her talking guitar would tell the tale.

Author's Note

Sister Rosetta Tharpe was a musician whose sound changed music history.

Born in the rural town of Cotton Plant, Arkansas, on March 20, 1915, Tharpe attended the Church of God in Christ with her mother, Katie Bell Nubin, known as Mother Bell. Mother Bell was a preacher at church and also sang and played the mandolin and piano. Rosetta was surrounded by music both in church and at home.

Rosetta picked up the acoustic guitar at the age of four and mastered it by the time she was six. Even as a child, she would join her mother onstage, at church, and as part

Sister Rosetta Tharpe at Wilbraham Road station in Manchester, England, filming the Granada Television special *The Blues and Gospel Train,* May 7, 1964.

of Mother Bell's evangelical music group, which traveled the country singing, playing, and preaching.

In the early 1920s, Rosetta and her mother left the South and moved to Chicago. As she grew up, the music from her childhood and the music of the city—blues, jazz, gospel—came together to influence Rosetta's guitar-playing style, creating a new sound that was all her own. People exclaimed that she could make her guitar "talk" as she used a unique fingerpicking style that hadn't been seen before.

In 1938, Rosetta—now a young woman—and her mother moved to New York City. There, she made her first record of gospel songs. The song "Rock Me" blended gospel and popular music and became an instant hit. Many future rock and roll and country stars, such as Elvis Presley, Jerry Lee Lewis, Johnny Cash, and Little Richard, said it influenced their musical styles.

Rosetta's reputation as a trailblazing musician spread, and she played at famous venues, such as the

Cotton Club and the Apollo. But being a woman guitarist was unusual in those days. Some gospel fans disapproved of her performing in nightclubs. And when she toured, many hotels and restaurants were still segregated, and she was forced to sleep on the tour bus and enter restaurants from the back door because she was Black.

Despite these setbacks, Rosetta loved to put on a show. Today, watching videos of her onstage is captivating. Bliss pours off her, flowing around the venue and mesmerizing everyone within earshot.

In 1944, Rosetta recorded the song "Strange Things Happening Every Day," which became the first gospel song to appear on the *Billboard* chart devoted to rhythm and blues music. People have called this the first rock and roll record.

So what happened? Why have so many people not heard of Sister Rosetta Tharpe? And why didn't she get credit for creating the sound that became rock and roll?

In the 1950s, when rock and roll was becoming popular, Rosetta was middle-aged. Rock and roll musicians were mostly white men, and Rosetta's contribution to their sound was mostly forgotten.

But over the decades, fans who knew of her music persisted in trying to keep her reputation alive. In 2018, over a hundred years after she was born, Sister Rosetta Tharpe's impact on popular music was finally recognized and honored, and she was inducted into the Rock & Roll Hall of Fame.

I wrote *Little Rosetta and the Talking Guitar* to celebrate Sister Rosetta Tharpe's early love of music. This story is an imagining of how Little Rosetta observed her environment and was inspired by the sounds around her, putting her heart, determination, and triumph on full display. The guitar was an extension of her. My hope is that children who read this story can see their reflection in Little Rosetta's curious eyes and bold style as they find their own rhythm in life.